Pros and Cons
HEALTH AND MEDICINE
The Impact of Science and Technology

Anne Rooney

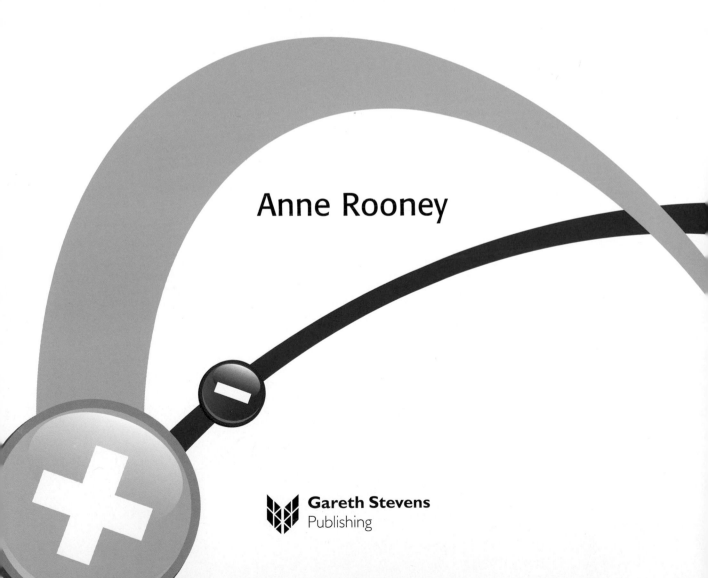

Gareth Stevens
Publishing

Please visit our web site at: www.garethstevens.com.
For a free color catalog describing Gareth Stevens Publishing's list of high-quality books, call 1-800-542-2595 (USA) or 1-800-387-3178 (Canada). Gareth Stevens Publishing's fax: 1-877-545-2596

Library of Congress Cataloging-in-Publication Data

Rooney, Anne.
   Health and medicine : the impact of science and technology / by Anne Rooney.
      p. cm. — (Pros and cons)
   Includes bibliographical references and index.
   ISBN-10: 1-4339-1988-5   ISBN-13: 978-1-4339-1988-6   (lib. bdg.)
   1. Medical innovations—Juvenile literature.
   2. Medicine—Juvenile literature. 3. Health—Juvenile literature. I. Title.
R855.4.R66   2010
610—dc22   2008054133

This North American edition published in 2010 by Gareth Stevens Publishing under license from Arcturus Publishing Limited.
Gareth Stevens Publishing
A Weekly Reader® Company
1 Reader's Digest Road
Pleasantville, NY 10570-7000 USA

Copyright © 2009 Arcturus Publishing Limited
Produced by Arcturus Publishing Limited
26/27 Bickels Yard
151–153 Bermondsey Street
London SE1 3HA

Gareth Stevens Executive Managing Editor: Lisa M. Herrington
Gareth Stevens Editors: Jayne Keedle, Joann Jovinelly
Gareth Stevens Senior Designer: Keith Plechaty

Series Concept: Alex Woolf
Editor and Picture Researcher: Nicola Barber
Cover Design: Phipps Design
Consultant: Mike Kent

Picture Credits: Corbis: 4, 22, 38 (Bettmann), 10 (Stapleton Collection), 15 (Chen Xiaowei/Xinhua Press), 24 (Franco Tanel/epa), 43 (CHU Amiens/epa), 44 (Jim Craigmyle), 46 (Wolfgang Langenstrassen/dpa), 48 (Pallava Bagla); Science Photo Library: Cover (David Mack), 7, 58 (Peter Menzel), 8, 36 (Antonia Reeve), 12 (Dr. P. Marazzi), 17 (CDC), 18 (Steve Gschmeissner), 27 (Andrew Leonard), 29 (Pascal Goetgheluck), 30 (Volker Steger), 40 (Philippe Plailly), 56 (Coneyl Jay); Shutterstock: 16 (Sebastian Kaulitzki), 20 (Leah-Anne Thompson), 21 (Alena Yar), 33 (Dr. Carolina K. Smith), 34 (Simon Pedersen), 50 (Michael Taylor), 53 (Aaron Amat), 54 (AG photographer).

Cover: Computer artwork illustrates in vitro fertilization (IVF), showing human egg cells in test tubes.

Every attempt has been made to clear copyright. Should there be any inadvertent omission, please apply to the publisher for rectification.

Printed in the United States

1 2 3 4 5 6 7 8 9 15 14 13 12 11 10 09

CONTENTS

CHAPTER 1
Science and Medicine   4

CHAPTER 2
High-Tech Hospitals   6

CHAPTER 3
Superhumans   12

CHAPTER 4
Fighting Disease   16

CHAPTER 5
Genetics   26

CHAPTER 6
Looking Inside the Body   32

CHAPTER 7
Organ Transplants   38

CHAPTER 8
Public and Private Health   44

CHAPTER 9
Changing Lifestyles   50

CHAPTER 10
Meeting New Challenges   58

Glossary   60
Further Information   63
Index   64

Science and Medicine

Developments in science and technology have been quickly adopted by medical science. New discoveries in disciplines ranging from space exploration to robotics are often applied to medicine, helping doctors both to prolong life and improve its quality.

Early Progress

The foundations of modern medicine were laid hundreds of years ago. The development of magnifying lenses in 1590 led to the invention of the microscope. For the first time, scientists could see that there are tiny living things — microorganisms — swarming all around us, and that our own bodies are made up of cells of different types. In 1865, the French

In 1865, Joseph Lister began using a spray of carbolic acid to kill germs during operations.

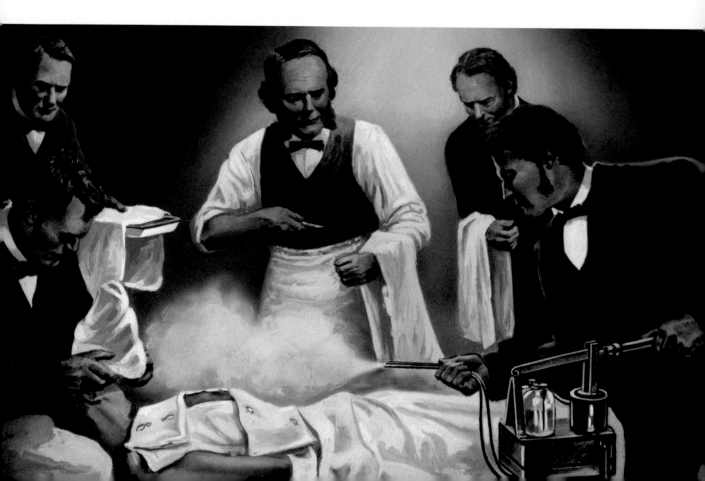

scientist Louis Pasteur discovered that microorganisms can cause disease. His discovery launched a new era in medical science.

Throughout history, medical technologies have brought breakthroughs in diagnosing and treating disease. The stethoscope was invented in France by René-Théophile-Hyacinthe Laënnec in 1816, allowing doctors to listen to sounds inside the body. The English physician Thomas Clifford Allbutt invented the first medical thermometer, to measure the body's temperature, in 1866. Those two inventions revolutionized medical care.

The development of anesthetics in the nineteenth century gave surgeons a way to numb pain. By making patients unconscious during surgery, or by numbing a specific part of the body, surgeons could operate more slowly and carefully on patients than before. With anesthesia, medical professionals developed refined surgical skills, carrying out increasingly complex and delicate procedures.

Technology and Medicine Advance Together

Since the early twentieth century, medical science has advanced at an ever-accelerating pace, making use of nearly every new scientific and technical discovery. Recent studies of the atoms that make up matter, and of the small particles inside those atoms, have led to imaging technology that allows doctors to see inside the body without surgery. The most recent developments in robotics have led to improved surgical procedures. Breakthroughs in the understanding of genetic inheritance and the chemistry of life have enabled scientists to manipulate genes and even diseases themselves. Every advancement takes people closer to achieving the age-old goal of humans — to live longer and healthier lives.

VIEWPOINT

Computers And Medicine

Computers have revolutionized many aspects of science. In medicine, the Internet is affecting how care is delivered by hospitals, physicians, and healthcare centers:

"In the next ten years we can expect … telesurgery [surgery using robotic tools controlled by a surgeon over the Internet] in … mainstream clinical practice … [and] integrated electronic health records. The challenge for health professionals is to harness the new power at their disposal for the benefit of their patients."

(Hugo Agius-Muscat, Director of Health Information, Republic of Malta, an island nation located south of Italy)

CHAPTER 2

High-Tech Hospitals

Two hundred years ago, an operating room was a horrifying place. Strong assistants held the patient down while the surgeon operated without an anesthetic in unsterilized conditions. If the patient survived the shock of the ordeal, he or she had a good chance of dying from infection. Modern surgery began with the arrival of anesthetics and germ-killing antiseptics more than 150 years ago. In the 1840s, dentists and surgeons began to use fumes from ether to lull patients to sleep during surgery. A more powerful anesthetic, chloroform, was first used in Edinburgh, Scotland, in 1847.

That same year, Hungarian doctor Ignaz Philipp Semmelweis observed that doctors who washed their hands between conducting autopsies, or examinations of dead bodies, and delivering babies cut the death rate among new mothers. In 1865, English doctor Joseph Lister was the first surgeon to use carbolic acid, which kills bacteria, to sterilize instruments.

Machines in the Operating Room

Today, an operating room is a sterile, germ-free environment packed with advanced technology to help the surgical team and the patient. During an operation, the patient's vital signs — his or her breathing, heart rate, and blood pressure — are carefully monitored by computers via sensors connected to patient. Computers also control the flow of anesthetics and any other drugs to the patient.

Telesurgery

In telesurgery, a robot performs an operation under the direction of a surgeon using remote control. The da Vinci robot has arms that duplicate the movements of the human wrist. The surgeon's directions to the robot can be relayed over the Internet. Because the surgeon doesn't have to be in the operating room, surgery can be performed by doctors who may be very far away from the patient. One of the first remote operations was carried out in 2001, on a patient in Strasbourg, France. The surgeon controlling the robot was in New York.

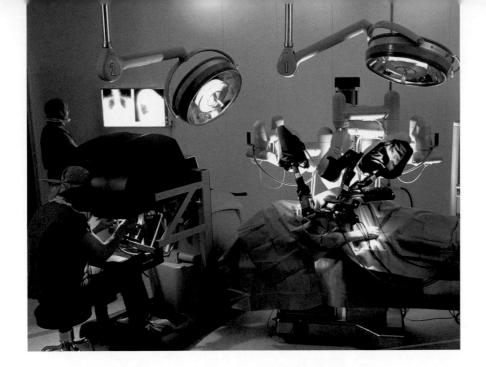

A surgeon operates using the da Vinci robot. The surgeon (*left*) can see a three-dimensional image of the inside of the body on a computer screen.

A surgeon may use advanced medical robots to help perform delicate operations. Machinery such as the da Vinci robot can wield tiny surgical tools with great precision. The surgeon directs computerized tools, sometimes working through a tiny incision, or cut, by using magnifying lenses. That system can also produce a computerized, three-dimensional (3D) image of the part of the body on which surgeons are operating.

 PROS: USE OF MACHINES

Computerized patient monitoring provides accurate data and enables skilled staff to carry out other tasks. Telesurgery gives patients access to surgeons and specialists who may not be available locally. In the future, telesurgery may be used to perform operations on patients aboard planes, ships, and even spacecraft.

 CONS: USE OF MACHINES

Some patients may be disturbed by the idea that their operation will be carried out by a robot, even though it is controlled by a human surgeon. Equally, some surgeons may feel that their skills are reduced or devalued by using robotic surgical systems.

New Techniques in Heart Surgery

Improvements in surgical tools and techniques have enabled surgeons to carry out more delicate maneuvers and more complex procedures. Surgeons can use methods such as laparoscopy, which involves making small cuts in the patient and passing a tube into the body instead of making much larger incisions through muscle tissues. Some laporoscopic operations can be carried out using tools fed along the tube (see page 37).

Heart-Lung Machines in Bypass Surgery

Open-heart surgery requires cutting into the chest. During the surgery, the patient's blood is routed through a heart-lung machine. The machine chills, pumps, and provides oxygen to the blood, performing the function of the heart and lungs, while the surgical team operates directly on the heart. That technique is used during heart bypass surgery. In some cases, patients have a quadruple bypass, in which all four main arteries to the heart are replaced with artificial tubes.

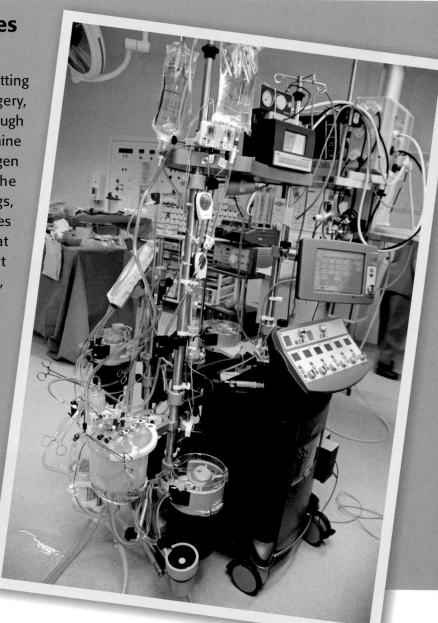

The heart-lung machine takes over the tasks of the heart and lungs during a bypass operation. It gives oxygen to the blood, removes carbon dioxide from it, and ensures it is the right temperature.

Great advancements in heart surgery have been made in recent years. Balloon angioplasty is used to treat coronary heart disease, when an artery, or blood vessel, in the heart becomes blocked. In a laparoscopic operation, a long tube is connected to a tiny balloon that is fed through a blood vessel in the patient's thigh. The surgeon guides the tube to the clogged artery, then inflates the balloon to unblock it. Alternatively, a tiny drill can be used to remove the fatty deposits in the artery.

Other techniques are much more invasive. The heart has four valves that control the flow of blood through the body. Heart valve surgery involves fitting artificial valves inside the heart to replace those natural valves that have stopped working. In heart bypass surgery, the surgeon removes the blocked or damaged section of the artery and replaces it with an artificial tube. Those operations take many hours and are very complicated.

 PROS: HEART SURGERY

Some laparoscopic surgical techniques are less invasive and can offer faster recovery rates for patients than traditionally open procedures. Such surgery can often be performed more quickly and economically, and sometimes the patient needs to be in the hospital only for the day of the procedure. Other surgical techniques, such as heart valve replacement, are much more complex. All heart surgeries can save lives. Many patients whose conditions would have been inoperable 50 years ago can now be saved by advanced techniques.

 CONS: HEART SURGERY

There is a risk that some patients may have a poor quality of life after their operations. They may have to take large quantities of drugs over many years, or they may need follow-up surgery. Advanced procedures are very expensive and are not always successful. Some people think the huge costs involved would be better spent on an increased number of less invasive operations for people who could expect a better quality of life after surgery.

Florence Nightingale is at work in a military hospital at Scutari (Anatolia, Turkey) during the Crimean War. Several modern medical practices began with her work at that time.

Intensive Care

Intensive care units (ICUs) are special wards for patients who are critically ill. The idea of segregating the neediest patients was first introduced by British nurse Florence Nightingale, when she was caring for wounded soldiers during the Crimean War (1853–1856). The first modern intensive care ward was established in Copenhagen, Denmark, by Bjørn Ibsen in 1953.

An ICU uses sophisticated equipment to monitor a patient's condition and keep him or her alive. Machines frequently carry out functions that the patient's body cannot manage, such as

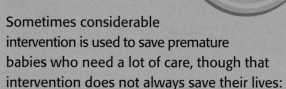

VIEWPOINT

Premature Babies

Sometimes considerable intervention is used to save premature babies who need a lot of care, though that intervention does not always save their lives:

"A premature baby is as much a member of the human community as anybody else, and deserves the best care that's available. By and large that care has been extremely successful. There are thousands going into adulthood who previously wouldn't have done so. There are some children at the extremes, for whom intensive care can't provide hope, and who will not survive. In those circumstances it's best not to start."

(John Wyatt, Professor of Neonatal Pediatrics, University College Hospital, London, United Kingdom)

taking on the task of breathing, assisting the heart, pumping the blood, or cleaning the blood of toxic wastes by kidney dialysis. A steady, carefully regulated stream of drugs keeps the patient free of pain and tranquilized. If a patient's condition takes a sudden turn for the worse, hospital staff can take emergency action — for example, to restart the patient's heart.

Neonatal intensive-care units (NICUs) care for sick babies. Babies born before the full nine-month term of pregnancy are called premature babies. They may not be fully developed and often need some form of medical treatment. Machinery in the unit regulates temperature, delivers oxygen, feeds the baby through a tube, and monitors his or her vital signs around the clock.

 PROS: INTENSIVE CARE UNITS

ICUs and NICUs have saved the lives of hundreds of thousands of babies and other people who would otherwise have died. Many more people have been saved from disabling conditions or impaired quality of life by the high level of care these units can offer.

CONS: INTENSIVE CARE UNITS

ICUs and NICUs can keep people alive long beyond the point at which their bodies would have naturally given out. Some intensive care patients have suffered such extreme damage that they are never expected to recover normal brain function. A patient with severe brain damage may not be able to move, breathe, or eat without technological assistance, and may not be able to think or communicate in any way. Relatives and doctors have to make difficult decisions about whether to suspend medical care and let those patients die. An extended legal battle in the United States surrounded the patient Terri Schiavo, who suffered brain damage in 1990. Her husband wanted her life support discontinued, while her parents wanted her to be kept alive. She died in 2005 when life support was suspended.

CHAPTER 3

Superhumans

People have long used simple aids to replace body parts lost to disease or in accidents. Wooden legs and hooks have been used for thousands of years, and eyeglasses were invented more than 700 years ago. During the twentieth century, technology moved beyond those simple aids to highly sophisticated technical replacements.

Inside the Body

Surgical advancements have enabled replacement parts to be implanted into many areas of the body. One of the best-known implants is a heart pacemaker. That device replaces or supplements the heart's own mechanism for regulating heartbeat. The first pacemaker to be implanted into a person's chest was developed in Sweden in 1958 by Rune Elmqvist and Åke Senning. Today, pacemakers also monitor and store information about the patient's condition. That information is sent wirelessly to a cell phone communicator, which the patient carries. The communicator uses the cell phone network to send updates to the patient's hospital, clinic, or physician. That means that the patient

Today, many parts of the body can be replaced if they become injured or worn. This colored X-ray shows a replacement knee joint. The two metal ends to the bones show up in cream on the X-ray.

needs fewer check-ups. The pacemaker also alerts healthcare workers if anything goes wrong.

About 30 million Americans suffer from deteriorated and painful joints, such as hips and knees. Many have replacement joints to relieve pain and restore mobility.

Some of the newest implants restore some hearing or vision to patients who are deaf or blind. The implants use sensors to pick up sounds or light and convert them to electrical impulses that are sent to the person's brain.

Bionic Eyes

A retinal implant of tiny electrodes can be fitted onto the retina — the light-sensitive surface at the back of the eye. The implant is worn with special glasses that have a digital camera and a laser. The camera captures an image, which is sent into the eye as pulses of laser light. Two microchips in the implant convert the light pulses to electrical signals. A set of electrodes in the implant sends those signals to the brain, where they are interpreted in the same way as normal vision. So far, the first retinal implants have produced only blurry images.

 PROS: IMPLANTS AND REPLACEMENTS

Implants can restore people's lives and enable them to be more independent. Implants that restore some vision or hearing help increase people's quality of life. In the case of a pacemaker, the implanted device can greatly extend a patient's life expectancy.

 CONS: IMPLANTS AND REPLACEMENTS

Implants and replacement joints usually work well, but there can be problems. Between 1990 and 2002, out of 2.25 million patients fitted with pacemakers in the United States, 66 people died as a result of pacemaker failures. Some electrical equipment and items that contain magnets may interfere with pacemakers, so patients must be careful to avoid such devices. If joints, pacemakers, or implants malfunction or wear out, the patient has to undergo further invasive surgery to replace or repair them. Hearing implants involve invasive techniques and may restore only partial hearing, which can lead to frustration.

New Limbs

Modern prosthetic, or artificial, limbs look very much like real limbs. Each prosthetic limb is matched to the individual's skin tone and body. Its "skin" is very similar to real skin in both appearance and texture. Many new prosthetics are bionic, which means that they use electronic and mechanical devices to mimic how the body moves naturally.

The newest prosthetics use "smart" technology to make them act more like human limbs. Computer chips take information from sensors to make the prosthetics respond just like real limbs. For example, a robotic hand can adjust the power of its grip. A robotic leg can adapt its way of moving to suit different terrain. Sensors in the fingertip or foot make those changes possible by communicating with a small computer chip in the stump.

There is ongoing research into biohybrid limbs, which will incorporate remaining biological tissue — muscles, nerves, and bone — into the bionic limb itself. Scientists are also developing limbs that make use of neurotechnology, technology that works with the body's nervous system. They are designing limbs that can be controlled by the signals that travel along the nerves. One method is to inject a tiny wireless microchip into remaining muscle that runs to the lost part of the limb. The microchip picks up signals from the nervous system and transmits them to the limb to make it move.

Future Developments

VIEWPOINT

Researchers are beginning to bring together the fruits of research in different areas to produce truly "smart" prosthetic limbs:

"We've got tissue engineering, neurotechnology, materials science, surgery. All of that work could come together in a biohybrid limb ..... My dream with this project is to [enable] someone who has lost an arm to brush [his or her] teeth or use a computer, or to allow someone who's lost a leg to climb stairs or ski again. I think we have the technology. We just need the courage to try it out."

(Ray Aaron, Professor of Orthopedics, Brown University School of Medicine, Providence, Rhode Island)

Oscar Pistorius of South Africa competes in the 200-meter final on his prosthetic running blades at the 2008 Paralympic Games in Beijing, China. Pistorius won the gold medal.

 PROS: SOPHISTICATED PROSTHETICS

Sophisticated prosthetics can greatly increase people's mobility and independence. The latest prosthetics look very convincing and may help stop people from feeling self-conscious about their bodies. Some prosthetics are specially adapted to an individual's requirements. For example, an athlete may have running blades for competing but more traditional prosthetics for everyday walking.

 CONS: SOPHISTICATED PROSTHETICS

Some patients find the connection between a sophisticated prosthetic limb and their body uncomfortable, and they may return to wearing a more traditional prosthetic. Tailored prosthetic limbs are very expensive to produce. That is a particular problem for children, because as a child grows it is vital to replace a prosthetic frequently. In countries where people have to pay for healthcare or health insurance, the latest prosthetic limbs are often too expensive for many to afford.

CHAPTER 4

Fighting Disease

Fighting illness and infection is the goal of medical care, and the impact of science and technology in this area has been immense. Our increased understanding about how disease is caused, how it affects the body, and how it is transmitted between people has come from a long history of research.

In 1854, a British doctor named John Snow demonstrated that the cause of a terrible cholera epidemic in London was contaminated water from a particular pump. But though he showed that dirty water carried the disease, there was no firm understanding of how that happened. When Louis Pasteur first suggested that microorganisms caused disease, he was ridiculed. The idea that tiny germs were making people ill was not accepted until the 1860s. Viruses, which are many times smaller than bacteria, weren't discovered until 1895. Since then, increased knowledge about bacteria and viruses has led to the development of new drugs and treatments.

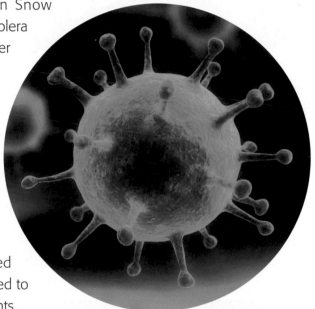

This is an artist's impression of a close-up view of a virus. Viruses grow and reproduce inside the cells of host organisms.

Bacteria and Viruses

To experiment with diseases, medical researchers collect infected tissue and isolate disease-causing bacteria and viruses. Dangerous microorganisms are kept in a sterile, secure environment and are handled with great care. Bacteria are independent organisms, and colonies can be grown and studied. Viruses can survive only inside the cell of an organism, called a host. Research into viruses has increased since the invention of the powerful electron microscope in the 1930s.

Virus Experiments

To understand viruses, scientists need to study them in the laboratory. That research involves handling some very dangerous materials:

VIEWPOINT

"Many influenza virologists [scientists who study viruses] remain nervous about creating and experimenting with a reconstructed 1918 Spanish flu virus, an extremely dangerous virus which disappeared from the world long ago. However, it cannot be denied that the information that has been derived from this experiment is exciting and represents an important milestone in understanding the severity of these highly pathogenic [disease-causing] types of influenza viruses."

(Dr. Jim Robertson, National Institute of Biological Standards and Control, Herfordshire, United Kingdom)

PROS: MEDICAL EXPERIMENTS

Laboratory experimentation with viruses and bacteria greatly extends our understanding of the diseases we have yet to combat. Such experiments have led to new treatments that both save people's lives and improve the lives of those who are living with disease.

A scientist works with a sample of the influenza virus that caused a pandemic in 1918. It affected a fifth of the world's population and killed about 50 million people.

CONS:

Keeping deadly microbes in laboratories can be dangerous, and some researchers have fallen ill or died as a result of laboratory accidents. The viruses that cause smallpox and Spanish flu no longer exist in nature, but vials of those deadly viruses are kept in laboratories and used for research. Some people worry that such viruses might be released by accident or be stolen and turned into biological weapons.

Medical Research

Once a treatment has been developed in the laboratory, the next stage of research often involves testing on animals. If that is successful, the final stage consists of clinical trials, in which the treatment is tried out first on healthy people, and then on patients.

Experimenting on animals is considered unacceptable by some people. They object on ethical grounds, or say that the response of an animal's body is not comparable to how a human body may react. Clinical trials on people may also go wrong. In 2006, six men who were taking part in a drug trial organized by a German company became seriously ill. The worst affected spent 16 days in a coma and lost toes and fingers as a result.

Coping With Cancer

There are many different types of cancer, but they are all characterized by abnormal cell growth. The rapid and uncontrolled growth of cancer cells usually results in one or more tumors. About 12 million new cases

This photograph, taken through an electron microscope, shows a breast cancer cell in the process of dividing.

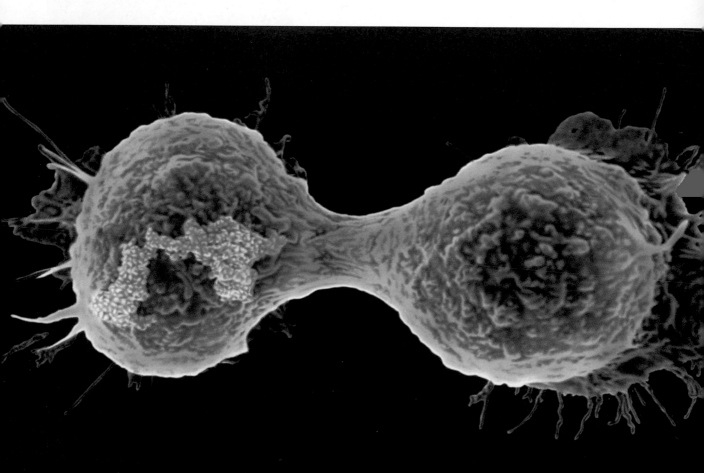

of cancer are diagnosed worldwide each year, and a half million people in the United States die of cancer every year.

Modern treatments for cancer can often cure a patient, or at least extend his or her life, if the disease is caught early enough. There are several ways to treat cancer. Radiotherapy uses radiation to kill cancerous cells. Chemotherapy uses strong chemicals to poison cancerous cells. Both methods have unpleasant side effects because they also affect healthy cells. Newer treatments try to target the cancer cells without harming healthy cells. They involve delivering drugs or radioactive materials directly to the site of the cancer.

The Fight Against Cancer

An experimental treatment for cancer involves using nanoparticles — particles smaller than a millionth the size of a pinhead — to carry anticancer drugs directly into cancer cells. The nanoparticles "fool" the cancer cells by appearing to deliver useful nutrients. Once inside those cells, the nanoparticles release strong drugs to kill the cancerous tumor.

 PROS: CANCER TREATMENTS

Cancer treatments extend lives and save many people from painful deaths. In some areas, extensive research and developments have led to a huge increase in survival rates. Since 1960, for instance, advanced medical care has increased survival rates for childhood leukemia, or cancer of the white blood cells. Once, less than 10 percent of children with leukemia lived. Now about 75 percent survive.

 CONS: CANCER TREATMENTS

In some cases, the treatment for a particular type of cancer causes as much distress as the disease itself and offers only a few months of extended life. For that reason, some patients prefer to forgo treatment and let cancer take its course. The high cost of new treatments means that they are often not available to everyone. News of breakthroughs in cancer research raises the hopes of all patients. However, some treatments will not work, and others will not be available for many years.

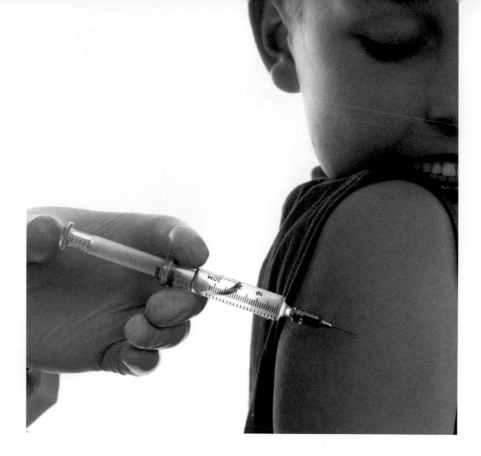

A physician prepares to inject a vaccine into a young patient.

Avoiding Disease

People can protect themselves against some diseases with vaccinations or by taking drugs or undergoing treatments that prevent disease.

Vaccination involves giving a person a very small amount of a disease-causing virus or bacterium that has been weakened or killed. The vaccine won't give the person the disease, but it will prompt the body to develop antibodies that will fight that disease. Antibodies are made by the body's immune system to fight infections and diseases. Once they develop, antibodies remain in the immune system to fight that particular disease should the body encounter it again.

The principle of vaccination was first used in Asia to provide protection against smallpox. But it was a British doctor, Edward Jenner, who in 1796 introduced a safe smallpox vaccine. He discovered that people exposed to the less dangerous disease of cowpox developed immunity to smallpox. There are now vaccines against many diseases. Children around the world are routinely vaccinated against previously common and deadly diseases, such as diphtheria and measles.

Besides vaccines, some medicines can be taken to prevent the development of disease. Aspirin is often taken by people at risk of heart disease, for example, because it helps to prevent blood clotting. Some drugs work by changing or improving conditions in the body to make it inhospitable to a viral or bacterial infection, or to prevent a disease from spreading.

 PROS: VACCINATION

Some diseases have been nearly wiped out by vaccination, and smallpox has been eradicated completely. Travelers can be vaccinated against diseases common in areas they are visiting. Healthcare workers can protect themselves against diseases such as hepatitis, which they could contract from the body fluids of patients.

 CONS: VACCINATION

Like all medicines, some vaccines can have side effects. Often those are minor, but occasionally people can become quite ill. If people are worried about a vaccine, they may refuse it (see page 47). Some diseases, particularly those caused by viruses, change so quickly that a vaccine is effective for only a short time. The influenza vaccine, for example, has to be redeveloped before every annual flu season.

Health in a Banana

Vaccines need to be kept cool and sterile, so taking them to remote and inaccessible regions of tropical countries is often very difficult. In response, researchers are developing new ways to deliver vaccines. They have used genetic engineering techniques to change the genes in an organism to create bananas that contain a cholera vaccine and spinach that contains a rabies vaccine. There is even a hepatitis B vaccine that can be carried in bananas, carrots, or potatoes. In each case, eating the food delivers the vaccine and gives people protection from disease.

Genetically-engineered bananas may be used to deliver cholera vaccines to tropical regions.

Alexander Fleming, who discovered penicillin, is at work in his laboratory at St. Mary's Hospital in London.

New Medicines

Since Louis Pasteur demonstrated the role of bacteria in illness, there has been great progress in fighting bacterial diseases. Pasteur discovered that bacteria could be killed by heating, a process called pasteurization. From 1865, British surgeon Joseph Lister used carbolic acid to sterilize instruments and operating rooms. Sterilization greatly reduces infection after surgery.

Antibiotics are substances that kill or prevent the growth of bacteria. Some work against only a few bacteria, but others, called broad-spectrum antibiotics, are effective against many. The first broad-spectrum antibiotic, penicillin, was discovered accidentally by Alexander Fleming in 1928. Since then, many antibiotics have been developed and are used for the treatment of both people and animals.

Antibiotics are effective only against bacteria, so they cannot be used to treat diseases caused by viruses. Viruses enter a cell and have the potential to reproduce themselves, then burst out and infect other cells. Antiviral drugs prevent a virus from breaking into a cell, or prevent the copies from breaking out. Knowing about the chemistry and life cycles of bacteria and viruses allows researchers to develop new treatments.

PROS: ANTIBIOTICS

Antibiotics are used to cure many conditions. The use of antibiotics has reduced infection after surgery or injury and saved millions of lives around the world. The use of antibiotics in farming has also helped to increase the yields of meat and dairy products by keeping farm animals healthy and productive.

 CONS: ANTIBIOTICS

The overuse of antibiotics in both humans and animals has led to the development of antibiotic-resistant strains of some diseases. Small amounts of antibiotic residue are present in many people's bodies, left over from treatments, and ingested through eating food from treated animals. Those small quantities have, over time, led to bacteria building up a resistance to the drugs. Infections caused by antibiotic-resistant bacteria include methicillin-resistant *Staphylococcus aureus* (MRSA) and *Clostridium difficile* (see page 50), as well as new forms of tuberculosis. They are all extremely difficult to control and treat.

VIEWPOINT

The Dangers of Overuse

An expert warns about the dangers of overusing drugs such as antibiotics and antivirals:

"We know from past experience that when we start using any antimicrobial drug excessively, that resistance to that drug eventually appears. Given the fact that there are very few new antimicrobial drugs being discovered, the message is that we really need to learn how to use the available drugs better .... It's easy to get into a mindset of just using them for any trivial condition. We are undoubtedly overusing these drugs."

**(Ronald Polk, Chairman of the Department of Pharmacy,
Virginia Commonwealth University, Richmond, Virginia)**

Planning for Pandemics

A pandemic is an outbreak of disease that spreads over a continent, or even the world. From 1348 to 1350, about a third of the population of Europe died of bubonic and other forms of plague, also known as the Black Death. Between 1918 and 1920, about 50 million people died in a worldwide pandemic of Spanish influenza. Flu pandemics recur at irregular intervals. In 2009, the World Health Organization (WHO) alerted countries about a swine flu pandemic after the virus mutated into a strain that passed easily between humans.

To prepare for and combat a pandemic, researchers examine body tissue from patients who suffered or died from pandemic illnesses in the past. In the case of flu, they use samples of the virus to discover how it attacks cells and how it could be controlled. Researchers use computers to predict how the disease might spread, how many people would be affected, what the social and economic impacts would be, and how health services could best cope. Drug manufacturers prepare vaccines in advance. They also plan how they would produce the massive quantities of drugs necessary to fight a pandemic. People at high risk, such as healthcare workers, would need to be vaccinated at the first signs of an outbreak.

A laboratory worker injects a sample of the avian influenza virus H5N1 into fertilized eggs. The goal of this research is to find a vaccine to protect against the virus.

PROS: PANDEMIC PLANNING

Advance planning helps governments and health services prepare for pandemics and encourages the development of new antiviral drugs. Government and international agencies work together to tackle what may become a global problem.

 CONS: PANDEMIC PLANNING

Publicity about possible pandemics can cause panic. In 2003, when cases of a deadly strain of avian flu started to appear in Asia, people around the world panicked. Governments, corporations, and even wealthy individuals began to stockpile antiviral drugs. That drained the world's supply, leading to shortages in areas where the drugs were already needed. A panic that turns out to be unfounded can also make people less likely to respond next time there is an actual public health alert.

VIEWPOINT

Avian Influenza

In Asia there have been some cases of a strain of influenza which affects birds, called H5N1, passing from birds to humans. The result in humans is serious illness and frequently death. At the moment, the disease does not easily spread from person to person but scientists worry that may change:

"The emergence of the H5N1 avian influenza virus … has raised concerns that it or another virus might mutate into a virulent [extremely harmful] strain that could lead to an influenza pandemic. Experts predict that a severe pandemic could overwhelm the nation's health-care system, requiring the rationing of limited resources."

(U.S. Government Accountability Office, Washington, D.C.)

CHAPTER 5

Genetics

Farmers have used artificial selection for thousands of years to raise more productive crops and farm animals, but with little understanding of how genetics actually worked. The first insight came with the work of Gregor Mendel, an Austrian monk who demonstrated the principles of inherited characteristics in 1865, after experimenting with pea plants. The idea that inherited characteristics were carried by chromosomes was first suggested in 1902. The structure of the chemical deoxyribonucleic acid (DNA), which makes up chromosomes and carries genetic information, was discovered by Francis Crick, James Watson, and Rosalind Franklin in 1953. The Human Genome Project, which aims to map the function of all human genetic material, began in 1990. Knowledge of genetics — characteristics that pass from generation to generation — has significant implications for medicine. Understanding genetics can help people predict or prevent disease and develop cures. Scientists are also beginning to understand how using genetic material may even help the body repair itself.

Stem Cells

When a human egg is fertilized, it begins to divide, making more and more cells. At first, those are stem cells, which have the potential to grow into any kind of cell needed to make a human. Later, stem cells begin to differentiate, making specific types of cells to form a heart, a liver, or skin, for example. The ability of stem cells to develop into other types of cells arms scientists with great

Growing Stem Cells

A supply of stem cells is needed for research and therapy. Instead of harvesting lots of stem cells, scientists grow a line of stem cells in the laboratory. A line begins with one cell that produces more cells, which themselves produce more cells. Once a line is established, it can provide an unending supply of stem cells for research or therapy. The first line of human stem cells was grown in 2006. In 2008, scientists grew stem cells for various incurable inherited diseases, which will help them find treatments for those diseases.

potential. For instance, it might one day be possible to use an injection of stem cells to regrow damaged nerves or heart tissue. For now, stem cells are valuable in research. Many serious medical conditions are caused by problems with cell division and differentiation. Researchers study stem cells to find out how those processes work and how they can go wrong.

Stem cells can be taken from embryos or collected from cord blood (blood in the umbilical cord), after a baby is born. Partially differentiated stem cells can be taken from adults.

This photograph of two human embryonic stem cells was taken with an electron microscope.

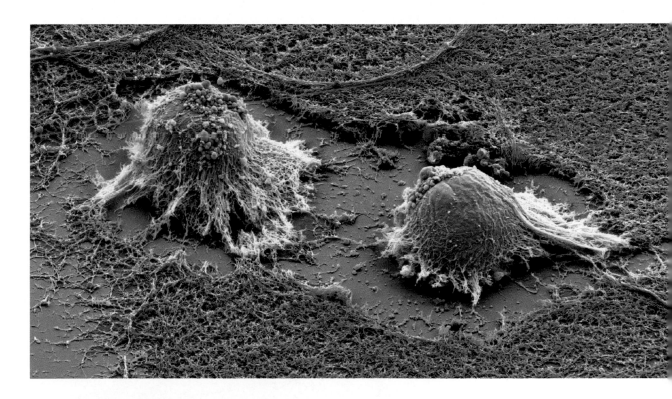

PROS: STEM CELLS

Scientists hope stem cells will offer a safe way to help the body mend itself. If the body grows new tissue, there is no risk of rejection or infection. At the moment, some blood diseases, such as some forms of leukemia, can be treated with stem cells obtained from cord blood. In the future, disorders such as Parkinson's disease and Alzheimer's might also be treated with stem cells.

CONS: STEM CELLS

Stem cells are most easily harvested from fertilized eggs. Such eggs have the potential, if implanted in a woman, to become babies. The use of stem cells that come from embryos raises complex practical and ethical problems. Research on adult and cord blood supplies of stem cells is less controversial. However, there are questions about how cord blood should be used, too. While some cord blood is stored in public banks, there are also private banks where parents can pay to keep cord blood from their child or children. Public banks are a vital resource if stem cell technology is to benefit the general population.

Genetic Screening

Until recently, people with a history of hereditary disease in their family had no sure way of knowing whether they would become ill — they just had to wait and see. Huntington's chorea is an example of such a disease. It causes disability and early death, but symptoms do not emerge until people are in their thirties or forties. Someone with a parent who has Huntington's chorea has a 50 percent chance of developing the disease. The exact genes that produce some inherited diseases, including Huntington's chorea, are now known. People who may be at risk can be screened to see if they have the genes that will lead to the development of certain diseases.

Sometimes, people pass on a genetic disease without suffering from it themselves. Cystic fibrosis is an example of that type of disease. When carriers plan to have children, they may choose to use in vitro fertilization (IVF). In that procedure, the eggs are fertilized outside the woman's body and the resulting embryos can be screened before they are implanted in the womb. Only embryos that do not carry the disease are implanted.

Saved by a Sibling

"Savior siblings" are babies that have been specifically chosen, using IVF and genetic screening, to provide tissue for transplant into a sibling who is suffering from a genetic disease. The new baby is healthy, and its tissue is a good match for the sibling. Often, a transfusion of cord blood is all that is needed from the baby to combat disease in his or her sibling.

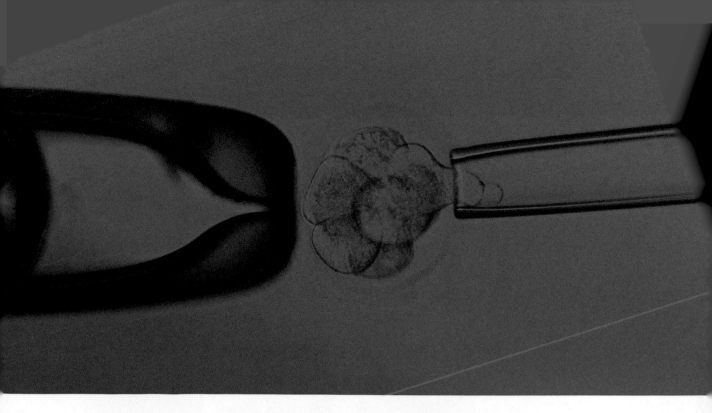

 PROS: GENETIC SCREENING

Genetic screening may spare people the agony of waiting to see if they will develop a disease in the future . If people know they are at risk of developing an illness, they may be able to take precautionary measures, such as adjusting their lifestyle, taking medication, or having surgery. Screening and IVF programs can ensure that people with a high risk of passing on a genetic disorder can make an informed decision about whether to have children who may later be at risk for developing that disorder.

CONS: GENETIC SCREENING

For some people, the certainty that they will develop an incurable disease is more stressful than the worry of not knowing. The knowledge that a person is free from one genetic defect does not mean he or she will be free from others. There is also a risk that genetic information will lead to discrimination. People may find it difficult to get work, or insurance, if it is known that they are at a higher risk of eventually developing a serious disorder or condition.

Scientists work in a plant that produces human insulin from microorganisms. The microorganisms are grown in the large vats shown here.

Genetic Engineering

Genetic engineering involves changing the genetic makeup of an organism, or changing the effect its genes have on the organism. There are several applications for genetic engineering in medicine. One important advance has been the ability to change bacteria and other microorganisms for use in drug therapy. For example, people with diabetes are unable to produce

Changing Genes

To make a genetically modified organism scientists take DNA from one organism and splice, or join, it into the DNA of another. That is called recombinant DNA. The production of insulin from bacteria, introduced in 1977, was the first commercial use of this technology. The human gene for producing insulin is spliced into the DNA of a bacterium. The bacterium is grown in a vat of nutrients. As it reproduces, it makes exact copies of itself, creating both bacteria and insulin.

insulin, a hormone that controls the level of sugar in their blood. For many years, the insulin used in injections to help people with diabetes came from animals. Today, it is possible to obtain human insulin in large quantities from a type of bacterium that has been genetically engineered.

Gene therapy, treating medical conditions by altering genes, is a promising new area of medical research. That technique would enable medical professionals to correct an inherited defect or change a genetic condition *before* birth. Turning off, or disabling, a gene so that it cannot influence the later development of an inherited disease or a cancerous tumor from growing is a treatment that may be in our future.

 PROS: CHANGING GENES

Using genetic engineering to make drugs such as human insulin in large volumes makes the treatment of some conditions cheaper and easier to provide. Other medical uses for genetic engineering include modifying foods to deliver vaccines or additional nutrients (see pages 21 and 52). It may be possible to reduce or eradicate populations of some disease-carrying insects by introducing genetically-engineered insects that cannot transmit diseases to humans.

 CONS: CHANGING GENES

Some people are concerned that genetic engineering may be ethically wrong, or dangerous to people or other organisms. Screening to make sure a child is disease-free at birth seems reasonable, but that technology also enables people to determine characteristics, such as gender, based on personal preference rather than health. We do not fully understand how genes interact with each other, so there could be unforeseen consequences to genetic engineering. The high cost of genetic engineering means that the companies developing techniques want to retain ownership of them so that they can profit from the investments they have made. That means that the benefits of genetic engineering may be available only to wealthy people in developed countries.

CHAPTER 6

Looking Inside the Body

When the German physicist Wilhelm Conrad Röentgen made an X-ray of the bones in his wife's hand in 1895, he began an era of imaging in medicine. Today, X-rays are only one of the many ways of seeing inside a patient's body.

Imaging Technologies

X-rays are routinely used to provide images of bones that are broken or diseased. Chest X-rays help diagnose pneumonia and lung cancer. Computerized axial tomography (CAT) scans and magnetic resonance imaging (MRI) are used to take pictures of soft tissue. CAT scanners use X-rays together with a chemical contrast agent that penetrates different tissues to different degrees. A machine rotates around the body, collecting images from X-rays that pass through the body. A computer then builds a three-dimensional (3D) picture from those images. The first CAT scan of a patient's brain took place in 1972.

An MRI scanner uses a strong magnetic field to create images of the body. MRI scans are widely used to diagnose damage to the brain, muscles, and the heart and blood that make up the cardiovascular system, and to look at cancers. The first MRI scan was produced in 1977.

MRI Scanner

The MRI scanner is used to get a picture of soft tissue, such as muscles and organs. It uses a very strong magnetic field — about 60,000 times as strong as Earth's magnetic field — to align the direction of hydrogen nuclei within the body. Radio waves are then used to change the alignment of the nuclei, and those changes are measured by a scanner. A computer can build an image of soft tissue in a series of "slices" in any direction from those measurements.

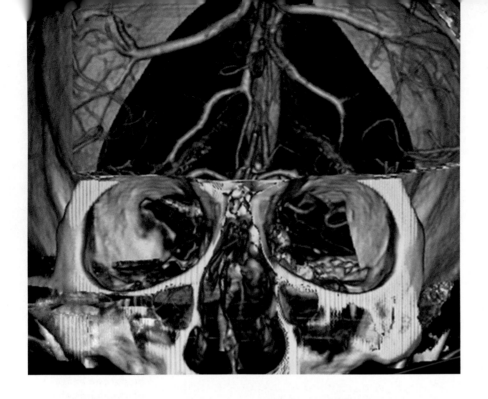

An MRI scan shows the blood vessels in the brain. Such images are often used to find aneurysms, or abnormally bulging blood vessels.

 PROS: IMAGING

Detailed imaging helps diagnose illnesses and identify damaged tissue or abnormal cell growth. Identifying such problems at an early stage can be crucial for successful treatment. Information gained about the brain from improved imaging has led to a greater understanding of how the brain works, and of mental illness and brain damage.

 CONS: IMAGING

Some CAT and MRI patients have a serious allergic reaction to the contrast agent used. The agent can also cause kidney damage, and is not suitable for all patients. People with a pacemaker or other metal implants cannot have MRI scans because of the use of magnetic fields, though newer implants are being made MRI-safe. An MRI scan can be uncomfortable. It is sometimes noisy and the patient has to lie still for up to an hour in an enclosed space. Many people experience twitching caused by the switching of the magnetic field. The MRI images sometimes reveal lumps that turn out to be harmless, but their discovery can cause stress for patients until the issue is resolved.

The Body at Work

A positron emission tomography (PET) scan measures body functions, such as blood flow and oxygen use, as they happen. That allows doctors to see how the body is working and detect any problems. The patient ingests or is injected with a substance used by the body (often a sugar) which contains a low-risk radioactive chemical. That chemical emits energy at a steady rate. The energy it gives off in different places is measured by a scanner and then translated into an image by a computer. The result is a detailed image of the inner workings of the body. A PET scan is often used to diagnose cancer

PET Scans for Alzheimer's

Alzheimer's is a disease that causes slow mental degeneration. A new technique for diagnosing Alzheimer's uses a radioactive or "glowing" dye and a PET scanner. The dye binds to a protein produced in areas of the brain affected by Alzheimer's. Those areas show up in red on the scan. It is the first clinical test for Alzheimer's. Previously, all diagnosis was based purely on assessing the patient's symptoms.

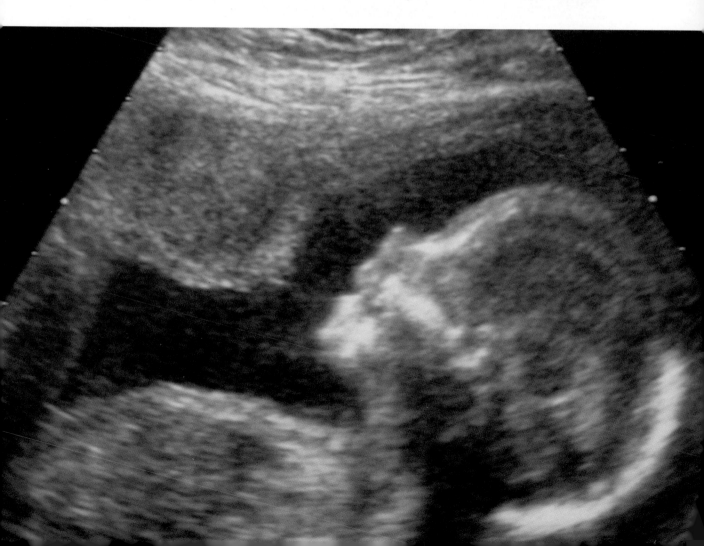

An ultrasound can produce an image of an unborn baby inside the womb.

and brain disease. It is also used in research to investigate how healthy bodies function.

Ultrasound and thermal imaging also enable physicians to see moving structures inside the body. Ultrasound sends sound waves into the body and creates an image from the echo of those sound waves. It shows the density of soft and hard tissue in organs, muscles, tendons, and the eyes. It is commonly used in pregnancy to check the position and development of the fetus. Ultrasound is also used by surgeons to help them guide fine needles through the body. That technique is often used to do biopsies, the process of removing cells or tissue for microscopic examination.

Thermal imaging, or thermography, creates an image from heat emitted by the body. Cell activity and generated heat are greater near cancerous tumors, so thermography is often used to detect cancers, especially breast cancers. Thermal imaging is also a useful research tool because it shows how the body works during different types of activity.

 PROS: ULTRASOUND AND THERMAL IMAGING

Imaging procedures can lead to the early diagnosis of conditions such as intestinal blockages and tumors. Ultrasound is useful to track the progression of a pregnancy and to diagnose any problems that may require immediate treatment or may have implications for the birth. For instance, ultrasound can reveal multiple fetuses, such as twins and triplets. It can also detect an ectopic pregnancy, which is when the fetus develops outside the womb and cannot survive. The images produced by those technologies have provided invaluable facts about organs and systems deep within the body and how they work together.

 CONS: ULTRASOUND AND THERMAL IMAGING

These safe technologies have few negative impacts. However, all of them can occasionally reveal symptoms that require further investigation that are often found later to be harmless. Additional testing increases the cost of treatment and is often a source of needless worry for patients.

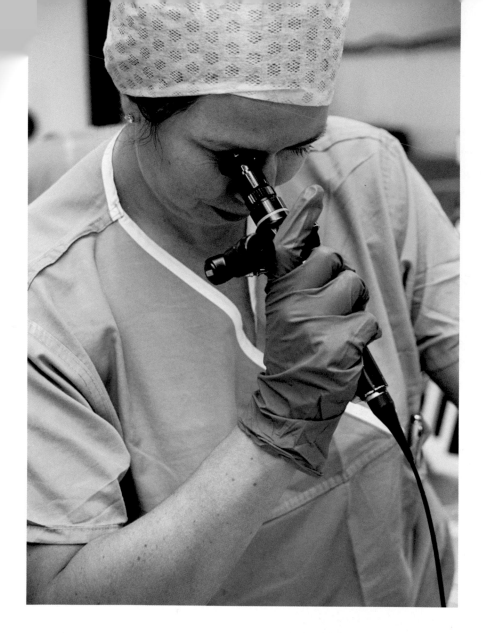

A surgeon uses an endoscope to see inside a patient's body. The endoscope has a camera and a light, so the surgeon can take photographs of internal organs.

Cameras in the Body

From the early 1950s, a British physicist named Harold Hopkins developed the technique of using fiber-optic cables to see deep inside the body. Hopkins finalized his design in 1967. The modern endoscope is a long tube that contains fiber-optic cables which take light into the body and allow doctors to view, record on videotape, or photograph internal

Super Skinny Endoscope

The newest endoscope, developed in 2004 by Australian researcher Martijn van Eijkelenborg, is thin enough to fit among blood vessels. It is only half a millimeter wide and is made from a single fiber with hundreds of holes running along its length. An ordinary endoscope is a bundle of fibers about five millimeters across.

organs. It is commonly used to investigate intestinal and gynecological disfunctions. To look inside the gut, the patient is partially sedated before the endoscope is passed down the throat.

A laparoscope is a type of endoscope with a shorter tube that is inserted through a small incision, often in the abdomen. In laparoscopic surgery, also called keyhole surgery, a surgeon uses small instruments to work inside the body through a very small incision. Both endoscopy and laparoscopy can be used to take biopsies, to retrieve foreign objects that have been swallowed or inhaled, or to aid surgeons in placing implants.

 PROS: ENDOSCOPY AND LAPAROSCOPY

Endoscopy has largely replaced the use of barium solutions to investigate blockages or lumps in the intestines. Previously, patients were fed unpleasant mixtures of barium sulfate, which appears on X-rays, and the abdomens were then X-rayed to reveal any problems. Both endoscopy and laparoscopy are minimally invasive and do not require the use of X-rays. They are a great diagnostic tool and can often be used instead of investigative surgery. Because laparoscopic surgery is less invasive than open surgery, patients suffer less pain and damage to muscles and skin and often need only short stays in the hospital.

 CONS: ENDOSCOPY AND LAPAROSCOPY

Organs are sometimes damaged by an endoscope or laparoscope. Patients are sedated for endoscopy but may suffer a sore throat and other side effects after the procedure. Laparoscopic surgery usually requires several incisions, so there is pain at more than one site and more than one wound to heal. Patients are often admitted to a hospital for only a day for laparoscopic surgery, and complications can sometimes occur after they have been sent home. Laparoscopic surgery also uses costly equipment and requires special training, so it is not available everywhere.

CHAPTER 7

Organ Transplants

Some damage to body parts cannot be repaired, but a damaged organ can sometimes be replaced. A surgeon may suggest that a patient undergo a transplant to replace a faulty organ. Organs for transplant come from people who have chosen to donate their organs after death, often from people who have died in accidents.

Heart and Lung Transplants

Experiments to transplant organs and tissues began long ago. The first successful transplant was performed in 1668 by a Dutchman, Job van Meeneren, when he took bone from a dog to repair a human skull. In 1967, a South African surgeon named Christiaan Barnard carried out the first successful heart transplant. The patient survived for 18 days before dying of pneumonia. The first heart-lung transplant took place in the United States in 1981; the patient survived for 5 years. Today, microsurgery techniques, heart-lung bypass machines, and

Surgeon Christiaan Barnard shows an X-ray of the chest of the first heart-transplant patient, Louis Washansky.

Scientific Breakthrough?

VIEWPOINT

Dr. Christiaan Barnard made this comment about the first heart transplant in 1967:

"[The heart is] a very easy organ to transplant. There will be much greater scientific breakthroughs in medicine, because the heart transplant was not a scientific breakthrough. It was a technical breakthrough."

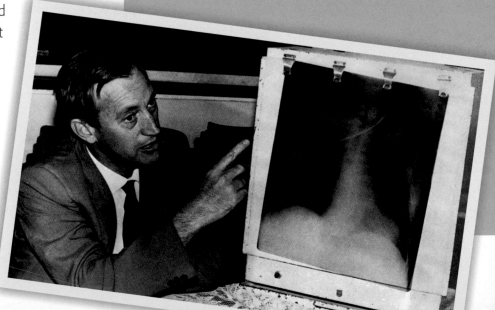

sophisticated antirejection drugs enable surgeons to replace the heart and lungs of a patient with an even greater rate of success.

The list of people waiting for donor organs is long, but the number of donors is fairly small. At present, there is such high demand for transplant organs that about 60 percent of patients die while waiting for a compatible organ. Using organs from other animals (most likely pigs) could end that shortage. The transplant of an organ between species is called xenotransplant. The largest obstacle to xenotransplant is rejection of the new organ, but genetic engineering may be able to overcome that.

 PROS: TRANSPLANTS

Transplants restore many patients to full health, and those people can often live active and independent lives after surgery. Transplant surgery has benefited medical science in several ways. It has furthered the development of microsurgery techniques and improved our understanding of how the immune system works.

CONS: TRANSPLANTS

The shortage of organs for donation has led to unethical practices in some countries, including the sale of organs on international markets and the harvesting of dying patients' organs without the consent of their families.

Patients need to take powerful antirejection drugs until the body has accepted the organ. If the organ is rejected, the patient must take antirejection drugs for life. Those drugs suppress the immune system, making people vulnerable to other infections. Sometimes, the drugs cannot stop rejection and the organ must be removed. The risk of rejection varies with different organs. The risk that the body will reject cornea transplants in the eye is low, for instance, but the risk of rejection is high for kidney transplants.

Some people fear xenotransplants will make them feel less human, or give them new kinds of infections or complications. Others oppose transplants from animals because of religious or personal beliefs.

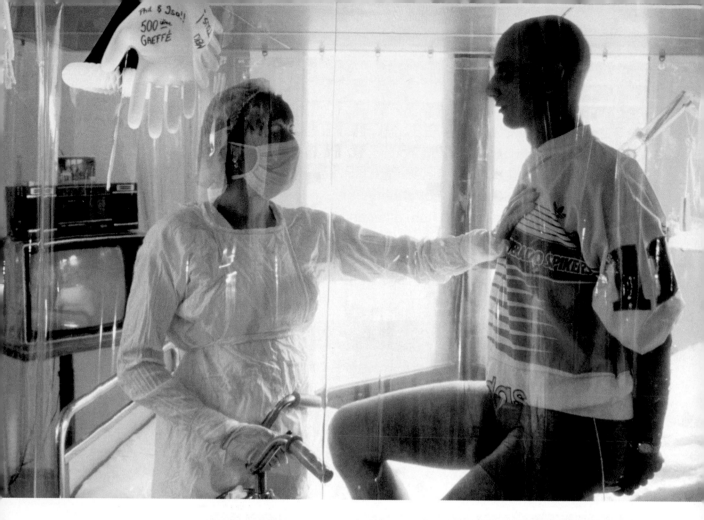

Transplants From Living Donors

Not all transplant donors are dead. For transplants that do not require a complete organ, a living donor is often used. Living donors can give skin, for example. They can give a kidney, as people need only one of their two kidneys to live normally, or part of their liver. The donor's own liver will regrow and more healthy liver will grow in the patient. Often, kidney or liver transplants are from donors related to the patient. Blood relatives are more likely to have compatible organs, reducing the risk of rejection.

Some conditions that require a liver transplant are caused by the patient's own behavior — such as damage from an overdose of acetaminophen or cirrhosis caused by excessive drinking. There is some debate about whether people who may be responsible for their condition should be equally eligible for donor organs as patients who are ill through no fault of their own.

Bone marrow and blood are transfused rather than transplanted. Bone marrow and blood are drawn from living donors, carefully matched to a

A patient who has received a bone marrow transplant uses an exercise bicycle inside his sterile room while recovering from treatment.

recipient, and then pumped directly into the bloodstream of the patient. Donated bone marrow is used to treat leukemia and other blood diseases. That marrow contains stem cells. With those stem cells, the recipient can produce healthy blood cells, replacing their own diseased cells.

As with other transplant procedures, tissue from living donors can be rejected, so the patient needs to take antirejection drugs. Patients receiving blood transfusions don't need antirejection drugs, but transfusions may carry other risks. In the past, undiagnosed infections have sometimes been spread by blood or bone marrow transfusions. HIV/AIDs and hepatitis have both been passed on through blood products. Today, all donated blood and tissue is screened for diseases and viruses.

PROS: LIVING DONORS

A living donor means patients don't have to wait for someone to die before they can receive an organ. Many people who are able to donate liver, kidney, or bone marrow to save a relative or a stranger feel privileged and pleased to be able to help.

CONS: LIVING DONORS

In most countries it is illegal to buy and sell human organs. However, the demand for organs is so great that there is an illegal market for them. Desperately poor people, often living in developing nations such as India, may decide to sell their organs. That puts their own health at risk and raises ethical questions about whether body parts should be bought and sold.

Split Liver Transplant

As well as splitting a liver between a donor and a recipient, the liver of a dead donor can be split between two patients. The liver may be split equally between two adults, or split so that one-third is given to a child and two-thirds to an adult.

Hands and Faces

Recent advances in transplant technologies, particularly in microsurgery, have made many new types of transplant surgery possible. In 1998, the first hand transplant was carried out in France. In 2008, a man in Germany received two new arms in the first transplant operation of its kind. The first face transplant took place in France in 2005. A woman who had been mauled by a dog had a transplant to rebuild her face. Transplants of exterior body parts such as hands and faces involve extremely intricate surgery. Not all transplants are to remedy illness and damage. People suffering from hair loss may choose to have hair follicles, the pores from which hairs grow, transplanted from the back of the head to bald patches. Skin grafts are frequently carried out to conceal scars or help to heal large wounds.

 PROS: VISIBLE TRANSPLANTS

People who receive transplants of body parts such as hands and feet have their mobility and independence restored. Those who have a retinal transplant are able to see again. People who need face transplants are very badly disfigured, usually by accidents, and have often had to endure stares and even unkindness. A transplant can completely transform the life of the patient.

 CONS: VISIBLE TRANSPLANTS

As with all transplants, patients have to take antirejection drugs and follow a strict regime to keep their new body part healthy. External body parts are on display all the time. Patients are constantly reminded that they have someone else's hand or face and some can find that very disturbing. If the transplanted part does not match the recipient's skin well, that problem is even more pronounced. The first hand transplant patient had the hand amputated in 2001, three years after the transplant operation. He could not cope with his body's rejection of the hand, the embarrassment it caused him, and his feeling of being emotionally detached from it.

In 2005, Isabelle Dinoire received the world's first face
transplant after being disfigured in an attack by a dog.

Face Transplant

A face transplant involves removing the skin, fat, and blood vessels
from the face of the patient and replacing them with those of the
donor. All the blood vessels and nerves in the new face are
connected to the patient's own face. The operation takes about
14 hours to complete. However, the structure of a face is
determined by its bones, cartilage, and muscles, so the patient's
new face does not look the same as it did on the original donor.

CHAPTER 8

Public and Private Health

Health is not just a private issue. Governments and health officials deal with the health of whole populations. They oversee public healthcare services and fund health initiatives. They educate people about health issues and promote campaigns to prevent illness. Today, some countries provide free healthcare for the whole population, funded by taxes. In the United States, people must pay for their own medical care or take out insurance to cover their health costs.

Computers and Health Care

In many countries, health records are stored centrally on computers. When people are ill or have accidents, their health records are immediately available to any hospital or doctor who treats them. Computers can also help doctors diagnose illnesses and choose treatments. Large databases hold information about a huge number of conditions, their symptoms, treatments, and prospects for recovery. A database can store far more information than any single individual can recall. Medical workers also use computers and the Internet to share knowledge with other professionals, and to ask for advice from experts in particular fields.

For individuals, the Internet provides a wealth of information about medical conditions. There are also online support groups where sufferers and their families can share information about dealing with an illness and its impact on their lives.

A doctor uses a computer at the bedside to update a patient's records.

PROS: COMPUTERS AND HEALTH

Instant access to computerized patient medical records can save lives. It can inform healthcare workers if someone is already taking medication, has a known condition, or is allergic to any particular drug. Online support groups are particularly valuable for people with rare conditions who may otherwise never encounter fellow sufferers. Some patients find details of new treatments that their own caregiver may not know about. Health services and hospitals put information online to help patients, sometimes reducing the need for people to visit healthcare providers to resolve simple issues.

 CONS: COMPUTERS AND HEALTH

Some people try to diagnose their conditions themselves using information from the Internet. If they interpret that information incorrectly, they may worry unnecessarily or neglect a dangerous condition. Self-prescribing and buying drugs online can be dangerous. Some information online is inaccurate. Some sites about eating disorders, for instance, promote the disorder and encourage unhealthy behavior. Many people worry that computerized medical records are at risk of loss or theft and that very sensitive information may not be kept securely.

Computerized Health Care

VIEWPOINT

In 2009, U.S. President Barack Obama spoke of his plans to introduce computerized medical records across the United States:

"This will cut waste, eliminate red tape, and reduce the need to repeat expensive medical tests .... It won't just save billions of dollars and thousands of jobs — it will save lives by reducing the deadly but preventable medical errors that pervade our health care system ...."

Immunization and Screening Programs

Immunization and health screenings are effective ways to reduce illness in a population. Screening programs may identify signs of illness at an early stage when treatment is easier, more effective, and less expensive.

Many new vaccines have been developed in the last 60 years, and some once-common deadly diseases have become rare in more

VIEWPOINT

Widespread Vaccination

To wipe out polio by vaccinating all children, healthcare workers need to penetrate even the remotest areas:

"Nigeria and India are responsible for the vast majority of new global polio cases. In Nigeria, we now have an effective vaccine to use and we've seen the start of improvements in vaccine uptake. These last pockets of unvaccinated children now need to be reached to achieve elimination in Nigeria and this in turn will have a dramatic impact on the prospects of worldwide eradication."

(Dr. Helen Jenkins, Epidemiologist, Imperial College, London, United Kingdom)

This baby is about to receive a protective vaccination at a clinic in Nigeria.

economically developed countries. Parents are encouraged to have their children vaccinated. Sometimes, extra pressure is exerted. Children may not be allowed to attend school unless they have the recommended vaccinations. Immunization programs are only successful if enough people are vaccinated. If most of the population is vaccinated, a disease cannot gain a foothold in the community.

Screening programs depend on affordable tests for common complaints. Those use tests such as X-ray and microscopic examination of cells to identify cancers before they produce massive tumors. The first vaccine to protect against cancer was administered in 2007. That vaccine is given to teenage girls to protect them against human papillomavirus, a sexually-transmitted disease that causes cervical cancer.

 PROS: IMMUNIZATION AND SCREENING

Vaccination programs are especially important in less economically developed countries where treatment is not always readily available. Scientists hope that polio will be the next disease (after smallpox) to be wiped out by widespread vaccination. Health screenings catch signs of disease early when conditions are easier to treat. That may mean that less aggressive treatments can be used.

 CONS: IMMUNIZATION AND SCREENING

Sometimes, anxiety about a vaccine can prevent people from using it. In 1998, a scare in the United Kingdom about the safety of the MMR vaccine, which protects children against measles, mumps, and rubella, led to many parents refusing it. The diseases soon emerged again in the population.

Widespread health screening for particular diseases is costly and inevitably involves testing many people who are healthy. It can cause anxiety, particularly when positive results are reported to patients in error, or when extra testing is needed. For both screening and immunization programs, participation is never 100 percent. Often, the people who do not come forward are those who are most at risk.

Mass Protection

Sometimes, governments take action to protect entire populations against disease. For example, some countries add fluoride to drinking water because fluoride helps protect against tooth decay. Around two-thirds of the U.S. population have fluoridated drinking water, compared with only 10 percent of the U.K. population. In some countries, fluoride is added to salt or milk. Similarly, other countries add calcium to white flour. (The calcium that is naturally present in flour is removed during processing.) Adding calcium to flour after processing restores a mineral needed by the body to build healthy bones and teeth.

To prevent disease, many countries spray large areas with pesticides to kill disease-carrying insects. In parts of southern Europe, spraying is carried out to destroy insects that carry infections such as dengue fever

A United Nations worker sprays a chemical to kill insect larvae on the island of Car Nicobar off the coast of India. The insects reproduce in pools of stagnant water such as this one.

and chikungunya fever. In some areas prone to malaria, the chemical DDT is sprayed to kill mosquitoes. Global warming is likely to mean that insects carrying dangerous diseases will change or extend their range, and be found in areas where they are currently not a threat. The spraying of pesticides will probably increase in the future.

 PROS: MASS PROTECTION

Water fluoridation reduces the incidence of tooth decay, particularly in children. That saves money on dental care and gives individuals the benefit of longer-lasting, healthy teeth. The addition of calcium to flour helps to reduce the incidence of weak bones. Spraying pesticides to kill disease-carrying insects prevents people from catching diseases and reduces spending on healthcare.

 CONS: MASS PROTECTION

Mass healthcare programs such as fluoridation and pesticide spraying take away personal choice. When fluoride is added to water, people have no control over whether they drink it or not. Too much fluoride can produce brown marks and pits in the teeth. People cannot choose whether they are exposed to pesticide spraying. DDT is a dangerous nerve toxin that is banned in many countries, including the United States. That poison is not permitted for purposes other than killing disease-carrying insects, because it can have terrible side effects on humans and wildlife.

Genetically-Modified Insects

In the future, scientists hope to create genetically-modified insects that cannot carry diseases. Those insects must be better able to survive than natural insects so that they replace them in the ecosystem. If that plan works, insect-borne diseases could be reduced.

CHAPTER 9

Changing Lifestyles

To stay healthy, we all need to follow sensible regimes of hygiene, fitness, and diet, and avoid overindulging in risky behavior. There have been great advances in our understanding of many aspects of healthy living, resulting from scientific discoveries and research.

Hygiene and Infection

Improvements in cleanliness and hygiene over the last 150 years have probably been the single most important factor in saving lives. The discovery that many illnesses are caused by microorganisms led to changing practices in hospitals and the development of new medicines. Today, hospitals try to reduce the risk of infection through rigorous cleaning.

Despite those measures, the development of "superbugs" such as methicillin-resistant *Staphylococcus aureus* (MRSA) and *Clostridium difficile* have become a major problem in recent years. Those bacteria are resistant to most antibiotics and are most dangerous to people whose immune systems are already weakened because of illness or surgery. MRSA and *C. difficile* are easily passed from one patient to another, for example, on careworkers' hands. In 2005, MRSA affected 278,000 hospital patients in the United States — double the number infected in 1999. One way to tackle those infection rates is to "deep clean" hospitals. That process involves not just surface cleaning, but thorough cleaning of infrastructures such as heating and air-conditioning ducts.

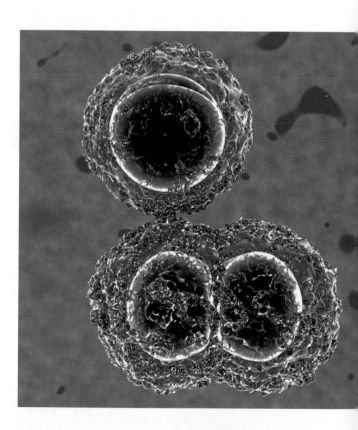

This is an electron micrograph of the bacteria that causes MRSA, a "superbug" that sometimes infects hospital patients.

PROS: HYGIENE

Improved standards of cleanliness in communities have reduced life-threatening infections. The availability of strong, antibacterial cleaners for use in the home and elsewhere has reduced the chance of infection. Increased awareness of the risks of handling food with dirty hands, or allowing cross-contamination, has reduced the incidence of food poisoning.

 CONS: HYGIENE

Some scientists have suggested that the increased cleanliness of many homes has led to a rise in the number of people with allergies and allergy-related symptoms, such as asthma. That is because the immune system develops by being confronted with microbial threats and then combating them. Cleaner houses present fewer threats and, as a result, people generally have weaker immune systems. The overuse of strong antibiotics has been blamed for the rise in hospital "superbugs." The process of deep cleaning hospitals to try to control those "superbugs" has also been criticized. Deep cleaning is disruptive and expensive and some experts believe it will have little effect on infection rates. They say that money would be better spent on more effective day-to-day cleaning.

Simple Measures

VIEWPOINT

The most important method for preventing the spread of viral diseases is very simple and can be adopted by everyone:

"To reduce virus transmission, attention must be paid to hand-washing and then … focus on cleansing surfaces and equipment shared by others, such as desks, tables, telephones, and door knobs."

(John Oxford, Professor of Virology at St. Bartholomew's and the Royal London Hospital, Queen Mary's School of Medicine, London, United Kingdom)

Diet

To be healthy, people need to eat a balanced diet — a range of foods that provide nutrients the body needs, such as those found in fresh fruit and vegetables and sources of protein, such as eggs, fish, and lean meat. In some parts of the world, food scarcity means that people are undernourished. In other areas, food is plentiful, but some people still have a poor diet. People may eat too much of the wrong kind of foods, such as carbohydrates like breads and sugar, and become overweight or obese. Even overweight people may be malnourished if they do not eat enough nutrients.

The food industry has changed rapidly over the last 50 years. Factory farming and industrial processing have led to the mass production of inexpensive food. Genetic modification means animals or food crops can be biologically altered, either to suit the needs of farmers and wholesalers, or to benefit consumers.

 PROS: FOOD INDUSTRY

Improvements in food production have made food more affordable. Technological innovations keep food fresh for longer periods, which helps people avoid food poisoning. In developing countries, genetically-modified food may help provide people with the nutrients they are lacking.

 CONS: FOOD INDUSTRY

The availability of affordable food has led to a huge increase in obese people. Obesity brings its own health risks, including heart disease and diabetes. Rates of diabetes and heart disease are increasing in many economically developed countries, even among children. Many scientific and technological developments in food production help producers, but harm consumers. One example is the use of hydrogenated fats, which extends the shelf life of food, but which has little or to nutritional benefit. Those fats increase the level of cholesterol in the blood and the likelihood of developing heart disease.

The Rise in Obesity

VIEWPOINT

It is not just the amount of food that people eat that affects their health and can lead to obesity:

"We tend to assess food intake by the size of the portion, yet a fast food meal contains many more calories than a similar-sized portion of a healthy meal .... Our bodies were never designed to cope with the very energy-dense foods consumed in the West and this is contributing to a major rise in obesity."

(Andrew Prentice, Professor of International Nutrition, School of Hygiene and Tropical Medicine, London, United Kingdom)

People often become overweight or obese as a result of an unhealthy diet.

Research and Campaigns

Education plays an important role in the improvement of health. The discovery that smoking cigarettes damages health was first made in the 1950s, and campaigns to warn people of those risks have existed since the 1960s. Research into the effects of alcohol on unborn babies has led to public warnings that pregnant women should not drink. The discovery of HIV/AIDs, and the fact that the virus is transmitted in body fluids, resulted in education campaigns to promote safe sex. Those campaigns inform people about unsafe practices that could put them at risk. Governments publicize the results of research into the risks associated with obesity, launching campaigns to promote healthy eating and exercise, and to limit alcohol intake.

Legislation relating to public health is often the result of scientific research. For example, research into smoking led to laws that required health warnings be printed on the packaging of tobacco products. It is also illegal to sell tobacco products to people under a certain age, and in many countries smoking is now banned in public places.

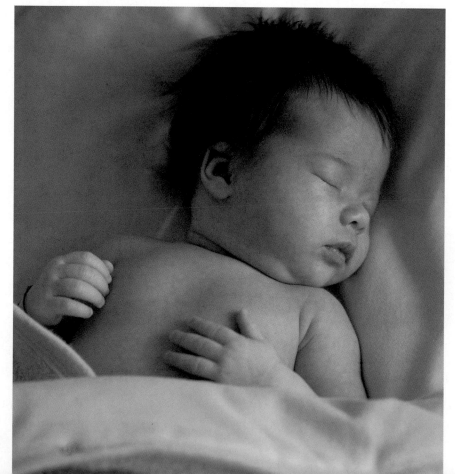

Research into Sudden Infant Death Syndrome (SIDS) led to public awareness campaigns to inform people about keeping their babies safe — for example, by putting them to sleep on their backs rather than on their stomachs.

PROS: HEALTH EDUCATION

When new discoveries relating to healthy living are successfully communicated to a population, people can make their own choices and take responsibility for their own well-being. Improved health in the population leads to decreased spending on healthcare.

 CONS: HEALTH EDUCATION

Health education programs do not always have the intended result. Sometimes, a campaign can seem to glamorize unhealthy behavior. Health education alone may not be enough to change risky behavior. People with limited incomes may want to eat more healthily, but may only be able to afford low-quality processed or fast food. As scientific research progresses, our knowledge about healthy living is refined, and sometimes changes completely. People are often confused by what they see as conflicting or changing messages. Some may decide that no information seems reliable and stop paying attention.

Too Much Information?

VIEWPOINT

Everyone is exposed to an endless stream of information about healthcare and health risks:

"A steady drumbeat of controversies, surprises, and scandals over the past two years — ranging from Vioxx [a drug treatment for osteoarthritis that was withdrawn after worries that it increases the risk of heart attack and stroke], obesity-related mortality rates, estrogen, calcium, low-fat, stem cell research fraud, among others — threatens to seriously damage the credibility of health research, creating a risk that the public will turn away from public health pronouncements."

(Jay A. Winsten, Associate Dean of Public Health, Harvard University, Boston, Massachusetts)

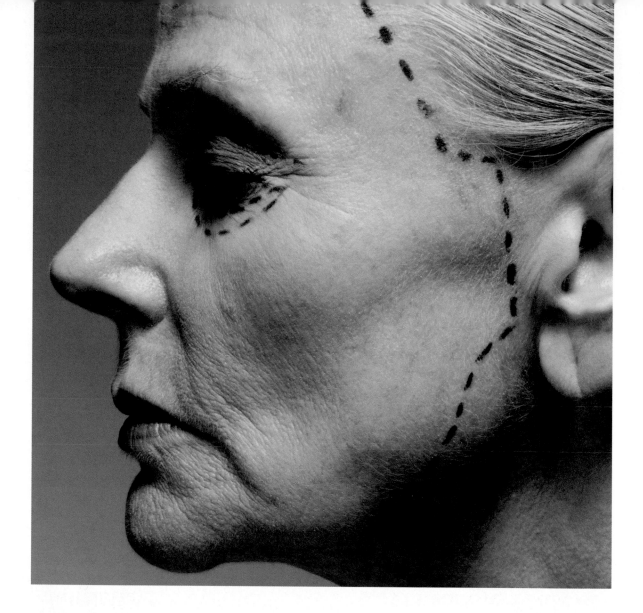

The Perfect Image

Increasing numbers of people are choosing plastic or cosmetic surgery to change their appearance to fit an ideal of what is beautiful. Plastic surgery began as reconstructive surgery, restoring the appearance of people damaged by injury or disease. The earliest known procedures, to rebuild noses removed as punishment, took place around 2,500 years ago in India. Today, much plastic surgery is carried out only for cosmetic reasons. It includes procedures such as remodelling the face, antiaging treatments, removal of excess fat, and the reshaping of the breasts. A large number of teenagers, particularly in the United States, are having cosmetic surgery. As techniques have improved and surgery has become simpler, many more people opt to transform themselves surgically.

The dotted lines on this woman's face show where the cosmetic surgeon will cut when carrying out a typical facelift operation.

PROS: COSMETIC SURGERY

Many people feel better about themselves after changing their appearance. In the case of surgery to reduce obesity, people are slimmer afterward and may adopt a healthier lifestyle to maintain their new look.

 CONS: COSMETIC SURGERY

Cosmetic surgery can mask deeper emotional or mental health issues. If people opt for repeated treatments, there is often an underlying cause for their poor body image, which should be investigated and treated. Surgical procedures may go wrong. Sometimes, people look much worse after surgery than before, and their health may be damaged. Implants that move around, go hard, or burst can cause discomfort or even dangerous complications for some patients. The long-term effects of cosmetic surgery early in life are not yet fully known. Young people who have surgery before they have finished growing may be at particular risk of problems later.

The "Perfect" Body

VIEWPOINT

Teenagers, and particularly teenage girls, are especially influenced by popular images of beauty:

"Teenage girls are acutely aware of and influenced by the lengths adult women are prepared to risk their physical health in pursuit of a "perfect" body. Modern reality TV shows that focus on plastic surgery may seem laughable and grotesque to older people, but they have a worrying impact on teenage girls in the throes of puberty .... While teenage girls are trying to establish a sense of their own value as humans, it is up to adults to teach them to be proud of their individuality."

(Andrea Scherzer, psychotherapist and eating disorder specialist, United Kingdom)

CHAPTER 10

Meeting New Challenges

The challenges facing medical science are constantly changing. New illnesses develop, old illnesses become resistant to established treatments, and changing lifestyles bring new health problems. Fifty years ago, HIV/AIDs had not been encountered, and the diseases caused by obesity were not as widespread. Even success brings its own challenges. By freeing people from some of the diseases which once killed many, we have created an aging population with new problems. The increase in heart disease and cancer is partly due to people surviving long enough to suffer from those conditions.

An aging population puts pressure on healthcare services and governments. In some places, experimental systems that automate some aspects of geriatric, or elderly, care are being used. to reduce the burden on struggling systems without reducing the care that patients receive.

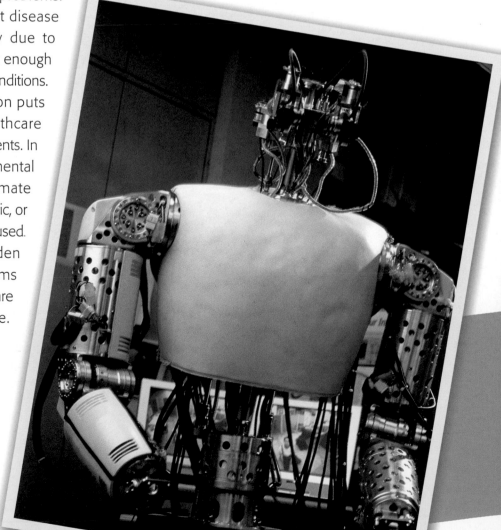

This humanoid robot has been developed in Japan. It has two cameras in the "head," touch sensors, and a microphone.

For example, an elderly person's health, movements, and interactions with other people can be monitored remotely using wireless networks. Such monitoring systems allow older people to live independently, while enabling their families and medical workers to make sure they are safe.

PROS: AGING POPULATIONS

Medical advancements have meant that people are living longer than ever before. Many of those people live healthy and independent lives. Many others keep chronic medical conditions under control with drugs or equipment such as a pacemakers or replacement joints.

CONS: AGING POPULATIONS

Not all elderly people are healthy and active. Many need constant care and attention. Conditions related to old age, such as stiffening or deteriorating joints, weak bones prone to fractures, and mental problems such as dementia, mean that some elderly people need operations, drugs, and specialized help. The quality of life for some older people is very poor. An aging population puts financial strain on healthcare services and society as a whole. Geriatric care is a challenge that societies around the world have to face.

The Pearl Robot

In the United States and Japan, scientists are experimenting with robots that can carry out routine care for elderly people, either in their own homes or in nursing homes. Robots such as Pearl, developed in the United States, will eventually be able to lift and carry patients when necessary, respond to smell, and help with simple tasks. They can remind patients to take medication, or assist them with basic activities such as hand-washing, if they need help.

GLOSSARY

AIDS (acquired immune deficiency syndrome) A condition in which the body's immune system stops working, causing patients to be vulnerable to other diseases from which they eventually die

Alzheimer's A condition in which brain function is progressively lost, beginning with memory problems and ending with loss of the senses and control of the body, leading to death

anesthetic A substance that makes a person unable to feel pain; anesthetics may act generally or locally

antibiotic A substance that kills or prevents the growth of a microorganism, such as a bacterium

antibody A type of cell produced by the body to fight disease

antimicrobial A substance that kills or prevents the growth of microbes, such as bacteria or viruses

antirejection drug A medicine taken to prevent the body fighting against and destroying new tissue, such as a transplanted organ

antiseptic A substance applied to tissue to prevent wounds from becoming infected

artery A blood vessel that carries blood from the heart to the body

autopsy An examination of a dead body to determine the cause of death

bacterium A very tiny, single-cell, living organism; some bacteria cause disease

bionic Combining biological and technological parts or techniques

bone marrow The tissue inside long bones where new blood cells are produced

carbolic acid A poisonous chemical that has antimicrobial properties; also called phenol

cholera A dangerous and often deadly disease that causes extreme diarrhea and dehydration and that is spread through water contaminated with the bacterium *Vibrio cholerae*

cholesterol A waxy chemical needed by the body in small quantities; too much cholesterol can lead to blocked arteries and heart disease

chromosome A structure found in cells that is made of DNA and protein and carries genetic information

computerized axial tomography (CAT) A scanner that uses X-rays and a chemical contrast agent to penetrate different tissues to different degrees

deoxyribonucleic acid (DNA) A complex chemical that codes genetic information through a sequence of chemical components, or building blocks

diabetes A condition in which the body is unable to regulate the level of sugar in the blood because of either a lack of the hormone insulin, or the body's inability to recognize insulin

electron microscope A microscope that produces a clear image at a high magnification by firing a beam of electrons at a sample

embryo An unborn, partially developed organism

ethical Relating to ideas of what is right and wrong

fiber-optic cable A very thin glass or plastic fiber used to transport light

fluoride A type of chemical that includes the element fluorine

gene The basic unit of hereditary information, carried in DNA on a chromosome and providing the information needed for a single inherited trait

gene therapy A treatment that involves making changes to genes or a person's genetic makeup

genetically-modified (GM) Changed by adding or removing genes

genetics The field of science that studies heredity (the way characteristics are passed from one generation of an organism to the next)

gynecological Describes the branch of medicine that deals with the diagnosis and treatment of disorders affecting female reproductive organs

hepatitis A condition in which the liver is damaged and inflamed

human immunodeficiency virus (HIV) A virus that attacks the immune system and can lead to AIDS

hydrogenated fat Fat that has been chemically changed by the addition of hydrogen in a process that converts liquid fats into solid fats

immune system The body's mechanism for fighting disease by producing antibodies

immunization The process of giving someone a small amount of deactivated disease to make them immune to (able to withstand) that disease if they are exposed to it later

insulin A hormone produced by the body that controls the level of glucose (sugar) in the blood

invasive Going into, or interfering with, the body

in vitro fertilization (IVF) The fertilization of an egg outside the female body

laparoscopy A type of surgery that involves passing a lighted tube through small cuts to investigate, and sometimes operate on, internal organs

kidney dialysis A process that performs the work of the kidneys by removing toxic wastes from the body, by routing blood out of the body and through a dialysis machine

magnetic resonance imaging (MRI) A scanner that is used to get a picture of soft tissue inside the body, such as muscles and organs

malaria A dangerous, often deadly, disease carried by mosquitoes and causing bouts of extreme fever

microbe A very small organism that can be seen only by using a microscope; microorganism

microsurgery A type of surgery carried out on a very small scale, such as stitching small blood vessels or nerves by using tiny instruments and an operating microscope

nutrient A chemical that is needed by an organism and must be taken from food or the environment

obese Very overweight

pacemaker A piece of equipment that is used to regulate the heartbeat

Parkinson's disease A condition that causes progressive deterioration of the central nervous system, affecting the nerves and brain

GLOSSARY

positron emission tomography (PET) A scanner that can be used to measure body functions, such as blood flow and oxygen use

prosthetic An artificial aid that replaces a part of the body that has been lost

protein A chemical with large molecules that makes up a major part of all organisms, from humans to bacteria and viruses

radiation Energy emitted by chemical substances as they change from one state to another, losing particles or rays of energy

retina The inner surface of the eyeball, with light-sensitive cells

robotics The field of science that studies and develops robots

sedate To put to sleep or subdue by lowering levels of awareness and response

smallpox A dangerous viral disease characterized by a severe rash, fever, and back pain, often leading to blindness, brain damage, or death

stem cell An undifferentiated cell that can develop into one of many types of specific cells, such as bone, blood, muscle, or skin cells

sterilize To make completely clean, destroying bacteria and viruses

telesurgery A type of surgery carried out remotely using computerized technology and robotic surgical tools

thermal Relating to heat

transfusion The introduction of blood into the body from an external source

tumor A lump or swelling caused by excessive growth of cells; tumors are either benign (harmless) or malignant (harmful)

ultrasound A type of medical imaging that uses the echoes from sound waves to produce a computerized image of the body's internal organs; ultrasound is commonly used to monitor fetal development

umbilical cord The cord that connects the baby to the mother's placenta while it is in the womb, and which conveys nutrients to the developing fetus

vaccine A preparation given to a patient to build immunity to a disease, and which contains dead or deactivated viruses or bacteria

virus A very tiny agent of infection that can grow only inside a living cell

xenotransplant The transplant of organs or tissues between different animal types, such as from a pig to a human

X-ray A form of electromagnetic radiation used to produce images of the internal body

FURTHER INFORMATION

WEB SITES

www.cdc.gov
The Centers For Disease Control and Prevention (CDC) is a U.S. government organization that offers facts and updates about infectious diseases around the world as well as their prevention and control.

discovermagazine.com/topics/health-medicine
Discover magazine regularly discusses current medical topics such as, cancer, aging, infectious diseases, genetics, and nutrition.

health.dailynewscentral.com
Daily News Central catalogs recent features from medical journals and arranges them by topic.

www.newscientist.com
New Scientist magazine often reports new breakthroughs and discoveries in medical science and technology.

www.nih.gov
The National Institute of Health (NIH) is an agency of the U.S. Department of Health and Human Services that provides information about the causes, diagnosis, prevention, and cures of human diseases.

www.nytimes.com/pages/health
The New York Times regularly features articles about medical discoveries, robotics, genetic engineering, and issues related to improving public health, nutrition, and food safety.

www.reutershealth.com/en/index.html
Reuters News provides daily medical information and is sorted by topic.

www.time.com/time/specials
Time magazine often covers new developments in medical science and technology.

totalhealthmagazine.com
Total Health magazine offers articles written by physicans that explain complex medical topics.

BOOKS

Ballard, Carol. *Cutting Edge Medicine: Fighting Infectious Diseases.* Franklin Watts (2007)

Campbell, Andrew. *Science in the News: Organ Transplantation*. Franklin Watts (2008)

Coad, John. *Why Science Matters: Finding Better Medicines*. Heinemann (2009)

Goldsmith, Connie. *Influenza: The Next Pandemic?* Twenty-First Century Books (2006)

Haugen, David M. and Susan Musser. *Genetic Engineering: Opposing Viewpoints.* Greenhaven Press (2009)

Lew, Kristi. *The Exterminator: Wiping Out the World's Most Infectious Diseases.* Gareth Stevens Publishing (2010)

Lovegrove, Ray. *Health: Ethical Debates in Modern Medicine*. Smart Apple Media (2008)

Rooney, Anne. *The Cutting Edge: Medicine.* Heinemann (2006)

Ruggiero, Adriane. *Public Health*. Greenhaven Press (2007)

Solway, Andrew. *Why Science Matters: Repairing and Replacing Organs*. Heinemann (2009)

Vaughan, Jenny. *Science in the News: Genetics.* Franklin Watts (2008)

INDEX

Page numbers in **BOLD** refer to illustrations and charts.

Alzheimer's 27, 34
anesthetics 5, 6
animal testing 18
antibiotic-resistant bacteria 23, 50
antibiotics 22–23, 50
antiseptics 6
antivirals 22, 23, 25

bacteria 6, 16–17, 20, 21, 22, 23, 30, 50, 51
Barnard, Christiaan 38, **38**
brain damage 11, 33

calcium 48, 49, 55
cancer 18–19, **18**, 31, 32, 34, 47, 58
carbolic acid **4**, 6, 22
CAT scans 32, 33
C. difficile 23, 50
chemotherapy 19
cholera 16, 21
chromosomes 26
computers 5, 6, 32, 34
    and health records 5, **44**, 44–45
    in surgery 5, 6, 7
cord blood 27, 28
Crick, Francis 26
cystic fibrosis 28

da Vinci robot 7, **7**
diabetes 30–31, 52
diet 50, 52–53, 54
Dinoire, Isabelle **43**
disease 5, 12, 16
    hereditary 28–29
    prevention 20–21, 46–49
    transmission 16
    treatments 17, 18–19, 22, 23, 27
DNA 26, 30

electron microscope 16, **18**, **27**
embryos 27, 28, **29**
endoscopy **36**, 36–37

Fleming, Alexander 22, **22**
fluoridation 48–49
Franklin, Rosalind 26

genes 5, 21, 26–31
gene therapy 31
genetic engineering 21, 30–31, 39, 49, 52
genetic screening 28–29, 31
geriatric care 58-59

health education 54–55
health screening 46–47
heart-lung machine 8, **8**
hepatitis 21, 41
HIV/AIDS 41, 54, 58
Human Genome Project 26
Huntington's chorea 28
hydrogenated fats 52
hygiene 50-51

implants 12–13, 33, 37, 57
    heart pacemaker 12–13, 33
    retinal 13
influenza 17, 21, 24
    avian **24**, 24–25
    Spanish flu 17, **17**, 24
    swine 24
insulin 30, **30**, 31
intensive care units (ICUs) 10–11
Internet 5, 6, 44, 45
IVF 28, 29, **29**

Jenner, Edward 20

laparoscopy 8, 37
limbs
    artificial (prosthetic) 12, 14–15, **15**
    biohybrid 14
Lister, Joseph **4**, 6, 22

measles 20, 47
Mendel, Gregor 26
MRI scans 32, 33, **33**
MRSA 23, 50, **50**

nanoparticles 19
neurotechnology 14
Nightingale, Florence 10, **10**

obesity 52–53, 55, 57, 58

pandemics 17, 24–25
Parkinson's disease 27
Pasteur, Louis 5, 16, 22
pasteurization 22
PET scans 34
premature babies 10, 11

radiotherapy 19
replacement joints 12–13, **12**
robotics 4, 5, 6, 7, **7**, 14, **58**, 58–59,
Röentgen, Wilhelm 32

Schiavo, Terri 11
smallpox 17, 20, 21, 47
smoking 54
Snow, John 16
stem cells 26–28, **27**, 41
sterilization 6, 22
stethoscope 5
surgery **4**, 5, 6–9, **7**, 12, 13, 22, 23, 36–37, 38–43, 50
    cosmetic (plastic) **56**, 56–57
    heart 8–9

telesurgery 5, 6, 7, **7**
thermal imaging 35
thermometer 5
transplants 38–43
    arm 42
    blood 40–41
    bone marrow **40**, 40–41
    face 42, 43, **43**
    hand 42
    heart 38, **38**
    heart-lung 38–39
    kidney 40
    liver 40, 41

ultrasound **34**, 35

vaccinations 20–21, **20**, 24, 31, **46**, 46–47
viruses **16**, 16–17, 20, 21, 22, 24, 25, 47, 51, 54

Watson, James 26

X-rays **12**, 32, 37, **38**, 47

About the Author
Anne Rooney has written many books for children and adults on scientific topics ranging from Earth science to alternative energy sources. She has written extensively on medical science. She lives in Cambridge, England, with her two daughters.

About the Consultant
Mike Kent is former head of the Centre for Applied Zoology, Cornwall College, Newquay, England, and the author of science textbooks, including *Advanced Biology, AS Biology for AQA,* and *A2 Biology for AQA,* and the *Oxford Dictionary of Sports Science and Medicine.*